W9-CLG-059

I want to be like you, Lord

From the Best-Selling Series

young readers

More than one million sold!

I want to be like you, Lord

Bible devotions and activities for girls

Betty Steele Everett

Augsburg
MINNEAPOLIS

I WANT TO BE LIKE YOU, LORD
Bible Devotions and Activities for Girls

Copyright © 1984 Augsburg Publishing House. All rights reserved. Except for brief quotations in critical articles or reviews, no part of this book may be reproduced in any manner without prior written permission from the publisher. Write to: Permissions, Augsburg Fortress, 426 S. Fifth St., Box 1209, Minneapolis, MN 55440.

Scripture quotations unless otherwise noted are from the Holy Bible: New International Version. Copyright 1978 by the New York International Bible Society. Used by permission of Zondervan Bible Publishers.

Photos courtesy of Images © 1995 PhotoDisc, Inc., cover; Bob Combs, p. 12; Jack Hamilton, pp. 26, 44; Mimi Forsyth, p. 30; Cleo Freelance Photo, pp. 62, 84, 106; Jean-Claude Lejeune, pp. 66, 88; Strix Pix, p. 102.

Cover design by Craig P. Claeys

Library of Congress Cataloging-in-Publication Data

Everett, Betty Steele, 1929—
  I Want to Be Like You, Lord.

  (Young readers)
    Summary: Twenty devotions applying scriptural principles to everyday concerns of girls, such as forgiving others, sharing, contentment, honesty, prayer, loving, and using one's talents.
    1. Girls—Prayer-books and devotions—English.
  [1. Prayer books and devotions. 2. Conduct of life]
  I. Title. II. Series.
  BV4860.E94   1984   242'.62   84-21565
  ISBN 0-8066-2112-5 (pbk.)

The paper used in this publication meets the minimum requirements of American National Standard for Information Sciences—Permanence of Paper for Printed Library Materials, ANSI Z329.48-1984.   ∞

Manufactured in the U.S.A.   AF 9-2112

00   99   98   97   96   10   11   12   13   14   15   16   17   18

Contents

About This Book   **page 9**

1   Hey, It's OK!   13

2   I'm Sorry about That   17

3   Happiness Is . . .   21

4   It's Not My Fault!   25

5   A Two-Dollar Bill   31

6   Branch Out!   35

7   What Do You Say, Lord?   39

8   Me? Love Her? Are You Kidding?   43

9   Make Her Help Me!   49

10   Playing by the Rules   53

11   Oh, Mother!   57

12   Need a Hand?   61

13   You Can Do It!   67

14   A Little Responsibility   71

15   Whose Side Are You On?   75

16   Watch Your Language!   79

17   Which Way Now, Lord?   83

18   I Wish I Could . . .   89

19   Let's Talk It Over   93

20   Thanks a Lot, Lord   97

21 It Wasn't Just Me   101
22 What a Neat Place   107

About This Book

God loves us. Because God loves us, he sent his Son, Jesus, to live on earth and then to die on the cross for our sins. Jesus died for your sins and the sins of all people. By dying for us, and by winning over death by rising again, Jesus gives us forgiveness. He also gives the world its only hope for life after death with him.

Jesus preached and taught for only three years on earth. Yet all during his life, Jesus showed us the love of God by being an example of how all who love God should live. Jesus loved everyone. Jesus forgave those who mistreated him. Jesus honored God and the world God had made. If everyone lived the way Jesus lived, this would be a perfect world. Everyone would love everyone

9

else and feel close to God. It would be the kind of world God wants.

Through reading the Bible we can learn how God wants his people to live. We can learn how Jesus lived. But we cannot live this way on our own, no matter how hard we try. We must know and love God and Jesus and rely on them to help us.

There are 22 devotions in this book. Each one emphasizes one quality that Jesus had and that we know God wants us to have. By reading them you can learn more about how you can live like Jesus and how God will help you to do just that.

These 22 devotions are short. You can read one in a few minutes. You can read them anywhere and anytime you want. If you already have a special time of day for devotions, use this book then. If you do not have a special time to spend with God, you may want to start one.

Some people spend their private time with God early in the morning before they get caught up with the "busy-ness" of the day. They set their alarm clocks early (you can start with 15 minutes) and spend that time reading the Bible and a devotional book and praying.

Other people like to have their quiet time with God at the end of the day, the last thing before they go to sleep. You may choose either of these times, or another time that fits your own schedule better.

10

Many people keep a "spiritual notebook"—a notebook like the ones you use for school but used instead for your personal devotional times. In it you can write down your comments, ideas, and thoughts when you read the devotions in this book or other books and the Bible. Write what you feel about what you have read. Write your own experiences that help you understand a verse or idea. Write which of the Action Ideas in this book you have decided to try. Write the results. Write questions you have, then ask those questions of your parents, pastor, or youth leader.

Living like Jesus did is hard. Without God's love we would not even think of trying, and even with his love we know we will often fail. That's when we must ask God to forgive us. God loves us so much he will forgive us and help us try again. God wants us to succeed at being like Jesus!

1 Hey, It's OK!

Jesus said, "Father, forgive them, for they do not know what they are doing."

Luke 23:34

Jesus was hanging on the cross. He had not been allowed to sleep for more than 30 hours. He had been beaten, spit on, and "crowned" with a ring of sharp thorns that made his head bleed. He had had to carry his heavy cross until he fell, exhausted.

Now Jesus could hardly breathe. The nails in his wrists and feet sent pain throbbing through his whole body every time he tried to move.

People were standing around the cross watching, but Jesus could not see many friendly faces. His disciples had all run away and left him alone when the soldiers came to arrest him. One disciple had even told the soldiers where to find Jesus. Only John had come back now to be at the cross.

From the cross Jesus could see the men who had done this awful thing to him. The people who had found Jesus guilty in a secret trial were there. The Roman soldiers who had beaten him before nailing him to the cross were there too. Some of them were gambling with dice to see who would get to keep Jesus' clothes.

Through his pain, Jesus could see and hear them. They were laughing and taunting him. It would have been easy for Jesus to curse these men. One of the thieves crucified with Jesus did curse.

Jesus did not think about cursing or getting revenge. Many times during his ministry on earth he had talked about forgiving people who hurt us. Now, on the cross, Jesus did what he had told his followers to do. He prayed for God to forgive the men who were killing him so painfully and slowly.

How could Jesus forgive these men who had been so cruel to him? He called on the love and power of God to help him. He knew that he could ask God to forgive these men only if he had God's love in his own heart.

Sue had worked hard on a super special leaf collection for science class. She was sure no one else had a project like it.

Sue had told her friend Lisa all about her project. She had told Lisa where she found each leaf, how she had mounted them, and what she would write about each one.

The day before the projects were due, the teacher held up a notebook for everyone to see.

"Lisa turned her project in early," the teacher said. "It's a beautiful leaf collection. This was a very good idea, Lisa."

Sue stared. Lisa's project was exactly like hers! A leaf collection had been her idea, but now everyone, even the teacher, would think it had been Lisa's.

"I hate her!" Sue sobbed when she was alone. "She stole my idea, but everyone will think I stole hers! I'll never speak to her again."

Sue was angry for several days. Then she remembered what Jesus had said on the cross. Sue knew that what the people had done to Jesus was a lot worse than Lisa taking her science project idea.

Sue asked Jesus to help her to forgive Lisa. She still felt a little angry inside, but she went up to Lisa the very next time she saw her.

"Lisa, you know the leaf collection was my idea." Sue said a quick, silent prayer for God to help her with his love and power. "But I want us to stay friends. So it's OK."

Sue did not know if Lisa would be angry or happy. She was surprised when Lisa started to cry.

"I'm so sorry, Sue. I knew it was wrong to take your idea without asking you. But I didn't have any ideas for a project, and I liked yours. So I— I just did the same one. I felt awful as soon as the

15

teacher showed it to everyone, but I didn't know what to do! I was sure you'd never speak to me again! Oh, I want to stay friends too! Thanks for forgiving me."

Action Idea: Are you angry with someone the way Sue was with Lisa? Is there someone you need to forgive? If there is, ask for God's love to help you. Even if you are still hurt by what happened, go to that person and say, "It's OK. I forgive you." Speak softly and be kind.

Lord Jesus, you know how hard it is to be hurt by people you love. You know it's harder to forgive them when they do not even seem sorry for what they did. But you told us we must forgive those who hurt us so that God will forgive us our sins. I want to forgive _____ (say the name of the person you want to forgive). Please help me to be able to say "I forgive you" the way you did on the cross. Thank you for your love.

2 I'm Sorry about That

If we confess our sins, he is faithful and just and will forgive us our sins and purify us from all unrighteousness.

1 John 1:9

The writer of this verse was the same John who was a disciple of Jesus. He was the only disciple who came back to be at the crucifixion. He is the same John who wrote the gospel book of John.

Jesus had been back in heaven many years and John was an old man when he wrote this book. It is really a letter to other Christians. Even though he was old, God helped John to remember clearly everything Jesus had taught. John knew he was telling the people the truth when he wrote that God would forgive our sins.

17

In the last devotional we talked about forgiving someone who has hurt us. But often we are the ones who have hurt others. Sometimes we get angry and do things we are sorry for afterward. Sometimes we think someone has hurt us, and, instead of forgiving them, we try to hurt them back. Sometimes we say things that others misunderstand and feel badly about.

Because we are the ones who have done wrong, even if we really didn't mean to hurt anyone, we are the ones who need to be forgiven. We are the ones who must say, "I'm sorry about that. Please forgive me."

Did you notice, though, that there was one "string" attached to what John said about forgiveness? We have to *ask* for it. It is not enough just to feel sorry about our actions; we must ask to be forgiven. We have to ask God to forgive us, and we must also ask the person we have hurt to forgive us.

If we first ask God to forgive us, then he will help us to say "I'm sorry about that" to the person we have hurt. Usually just saying "I'm sorry" is enough to straighten things out between you.

Anne wanted to go to a movie with her friends, but her father said no. "In our family the rule is you have to be in on school nights," he told her.

"You're just being mean!" Anne shouted. "I hate your rules!"

She ran to her room and slammed the door. Anne did not come out until she was sure her father had left for work the next morning. She had to gulp her breakfast and run all the way to the school bus because she was late.

That evening Anne did not speak to her father at dinner. She went to her room as soon as she was through eating. When her father knocked on the door and asked to come in, Anne said she was busy with homework.

Later Anne let her older sister, Laura, come in. Laura sat on the bed beside Anne.

"I know you're mad at dad," Laura said. "But you're making him feel pretty sad by not talking to him."

"I don't care!" Anne said. "He's mean! He wouldn't let me go to the show!"

"I know," Laura said. "But you knew the rules. Do you think dad should break them whenever you want him to? Remember the time I wanted to go to the city with the gang and dad wouldn't let me 'cause there weren't any adults going? Well, that was the rule, and he was right!"

Anne looked down at her hands. "I still think he's mean!"

"So you're hurting him!" Laura said. "That makes you the mean one! You're hurting dad because he did what he thought was right and best for you. Is that fair?"

Anne swallowed. "I guess not," she finally said in a low voice. "But what should I do?"

"Just say, 'I'm sorry, dad,' " Laura said. "Come on, I'll go with you."

When Anne told her father she was sorry, he smiled. "I'm sorry too, Anne. I wish the show had been on Friday night."

Then Anne's father held out his arms, and in a minute Anne was snuggled up on his lap. Even if she was getting bigger every day, it felt good to sit on her father's lap and know that everything was all right between them again.

Action Idea: Have you hurt someone recently? It may be a parent, a brother or sister, a friend, or a teacher. It's not easy to know you were wrong, and it's not easy to admit it to the person you have hurt. After you tell God you are sorry, go to that person. Simply say, "I'm sorry about what happened." The chances are they are sorry about it too. Then the whole thing can be forgotten.

You know I've done wrong, God. I didn't mean to, but I hurt _____ (say the name of the person you have wronged). I am really sorry, God. I wish I hadn't done it. I want to tell them I'm sorry, but I'm scared. Please help me to say it and to mean it. Please help us to get things right between us again.

3 Happiness Is . . .

*I have learned to be content whatever the circum-
stances. . . . I have learned the secret of being content in any and every situation.*

Philippians 4:11-12

Paul was a brave apostle for Jesus. Because of
him, Jesus' teachings were taken to the Gentiles as
well as to the Jews. But Paul had not always been
named Paul, and he had not always loved Jesus.

Once his name had been Saul, and he had hated
Christ's people. He had persecuted them. The followers of Jesus were afraid of Saul.

Saul was on his way to a city called Damascus to
put more Christians in jail. Suddenly there was a
bright light. Jesus spoke to Saul. Saul knew it was
Jesus and he believed. After that, Saul changed his
name to Paul. He changed his life too.

In this verse Paul is talking about being able to be happy in any situation that comes along. Paul had been beaten for preaching about Jesus. He had been put in jail. He had been shipwrecked. He had been hungry and cold many times as he traveled to tell people about Jesus and his love. Still Paul wrote to his friends at Philippi that he knew the secret of being happy no matter what happened to him.

What was Paul's secret? It was his love for Jesus and his faith that Jesus was with him wherever he was and whatever happened to him. Paul knew that Jesus loved him and would never leave him alone. Paul knew that even when he died, he would live forever with Jesus in heaven.

If Paul had not had his "secret," he would not have been able to live through some of the things he did. He would have been too discouraged and unhappy to go on with his work for Jesus. He would have quit and gone home.

It is hard for us to always be content and happy. Sometimes things happen that make us sad and dejected. That's when we must remember Paul's secret and make it our secret too.

Donna's father had been transferred to a new city many miles away. The family had to move there. Donna would have to go to a new school and a new church. She would have to make all new friends.

"I don't want to move, grandma!" she told her grandmother.

22

Donna's grandmother was moving to the new city with them. She would have her own apartment there.

"I want to stay here!" Donna said. "We've always lived here. All my friends are here. I don't want to leave! I'll hate it there!"

Her grandmother nodded. "You'll hate it if you decide now you will. But if you decide now that you will like your new town, you probably will. You know Donna, I didn't always live near you. When I was your age, I lived a long way from here. In fact, I've moved 15 times during my life!"

"Fifteen times?" Donna could not imagine moving so often. "How did you stand it, grandma?"

Her grandmother smiled. "I remembered that there wasn't any place anywhere that I could move that Jesus wouldn't come with me. Knowing Jesus was moving with me made it easier. I already had one old friend in the new town, no matter where it was. Then I started finding new friends. I looked around to see who I could help. I went to Sunday school and church the very first Sunday. Church is a good place to make new friends. Much of the church service was the same wherever I moved—like using the same Lord's Prayer and hymns. After that it didn't take long for me to feel at home wherever I was."

Donna thought about what her grandmother had said. "I guess I can do that," she said slowly.

"I forgot about Jesus being anywhere I go." Donna smiled at her grandmother. "I might even learn to like it better in the new city. And if we ever have to move again, I'll remember just how I did it!"

Action Idea: Do you have a friend who is unhappy about having to move? Or because she is sick? Tell them you are sorry they are moving or are sick. Tell them you are thinking about them and will pray for them. Write to the one who moves away. Visit or call the one who is sick. Remind them that Jesus is everywhere his people are.

Thank you, Lord Jesus, for being with us wherever we are. Thank you for never leaving us alone. Help me to remember that no matter what happens to make me sad, you love me and will help me.

4 It's Not My Fault!

The man said, "The woman you put here with me—
she gave me some fruit from the tree, and I ate it."
                                          Genesis 3:12

The man in this verse is Adam. The woman is Eve.
God was the one who gave Eve to Adam to be his
wife.

God had told Adam and Eve that they could eat
the fruit of any tree in the Garden of Eden except
one. It has become common to refer to this fruit as
an apple, but the Bible never tells us what kind of
fruit it was.

Satan came to Eve in the form of a snake and told
her that eating the fruit of that tree would make her
as wise as God. So Eve ate the fruit and gave some
to Adam. Adam ate it too.

Later, when God asked Adam if he had eaten the fruit, Adam did not want to take the blame for his own sin. First he tried to blame Eve. Then he tried to blame God. Adam told God that since God had given Eve to Adam it was God's fault. If it hadn't been for Eve, Adam would not have thought of eating the fruit.

Adam was really saying, "It's not my fault I did the wrong thing!"

But Adam did not fool God. God had made Adam responsible for his own actions, and he had to bear the punishment for them. Eve, too, had to face the results of her sin.

It is easy to sin. Satan makes the wrong things look as good to us as the fruit did to Eve. God gives us the choice too, just as he gave Adam and Eve the choice of good or bad. Christians must take the responsibility for their own actions.

We have an advantage Adam and Eve did not have, though. We know that we have a Savior who has already paid the price for our sins and who will forgive us if we ask him. But being forgiven does not mean we will not have to face the natural consequences of our wrongdoing. Sin always hurts, even though God forgives us.

Linda was baby-sitting with her three-year-old brother. Jimmy wanted to play ball with his big, soft, orange ball.

"We're not allowed to throw the ball in the house," Linda said.

27

Jimmy's face got sad. Tears started in his blue eyes.

"Well, maybe it wouldn't hurt to throw it just a couple of times," Linda said.

Linda threw the ball to Jimmy. He tried to catch it, but it hit his chest and dropped at his feet.

Linda threw the ball again. Jimmy lunged, got one hand on it, and batted it away. The ball hit a small vase on the edge of a table and knocked it off.

"Oh, Jimmy!" Linda checked the vase. There was only one small chip on the bottom. It did not show when she set the vase back on the table.

When her mother came home, Linda did not tell her about the vase.

That evening when Linda's mother dusted the living room, she lifted the vase. "My vase is chipped!"

"Ball!" Jimmy said.

"You hit it with the ball?" Linda's mother frowned at Jimmy. "You know you're not allowed to play ball inside! I'll have to take your ball away from you all day tomorrow."

Jimmy looked like he might cry. Linda swallowed hard. Jimmy had been the one who knocked the ball into the vase, but she had been in charge. She was responsible.

"It was my fault," Linda said in a low voice. "I threw the ball, and when Jimmy couldn't catch it, it hit the vase. I'm sorry."

28

"I'm proud you told me the truth, Linda," her mother said. "But you should have told me when I got home. You're too big to hide things like that."

Linda nodded. "I know. I'll save my money and buy you a new one."

Linda's mother smiled. "You don't need to. It's only a little chip. When we look at that vase, we'll both think about being grown-up enough to be responsible for our actions. And we'll remember that God loves us enough to forgive us when we do the wrong thing."

Action Idea: Think about Adam and his excuses the next time you start to say, "It isn't my fault." Promise yourself and God that you will not let anyone else take the blame when you have done something wrong.

I know I'm old enough and grown up enough to be responsible for what I do, Lord. But sometimes it's hard to admit that something is my fault—especially when it isn't always entirely my fault! Help me to be honest and brave enough to admit when I am responsible for a bad action. Help me not to let others be blamed for what I've done, even when I know I'll be punished for what I did.

5 A Two-Dollar Bill

Do to others as you would have them do to you.
                                                    Luke 6:31

   This is one of the most famous verses in the Bible. Jesus was preaching to a great crowd of people. These men, women, and children had come from all around that part of the country to see and hear Jesus. Some had traveled many miles. Some were sick and wanted Jesus to heal them. Jesus did heal them. He also preached to the people, and we call what he said the Sermon on the Mount. Both Matthew and Luke wrote down parts of it for us to read.

   Jesus talked a long time to the people. He told them what his followers must do. He told them what the rewards would be. He also warned them that they would not be popular if they followed him. Jesus gave the people rules to live by. He told them stories to illustrate these rules in ways they could remember.

This verse was one of the rules. We often call it the "Golden Rule." That means that if everyone in the world would act the way Jesus tells us to in just this one verse, the whole world would be different. It would be a "golden" world. It would be a safe, cheerful, and honest place to live. No one would hurt anyone else. No one would cheat anyone else. No one would be cruel to anyone else. It would be the kind of world God has always wanted it to be.

Living this verse can be hard. We often have a chance to take advantage of someone else, and we don't remember to think about how we would want to be treated if we were on the other side. The love of Jesus helps us to love others and serve them.

It was two days before Jayne's mother's birthday. Jayne had been saving to buy her a soft, light blue scarf. Now she was still a dollar short of the price.

"Ask your dad for it," Jayne's friend Sara suggested.

The girls were in the drugstore to buy some things Jayne's mother needed.

"Then it wouldn't be all from me," Jayne said.

The girls took their things to the cash register. Jayne was surprised to see her older brother's friend Bill working there.

"Hi, girls." Bill smiled as he rang up their purchases.

32

"I didn't know you worked here," Jayne said.

"Started today. If I do a good job this week, I'll get to stay all summer."

Bill counted out her change. He gave Jayne four bills and some coins. Jayne dropped them into her purse.

It wasn't until they were home that Jayne looked at her change. "Sara, Bill gave me too much! He meant to give me four one-dollar bills and he gave me three ones and a two-dollar bill!"

Sara grinned. "Now you have enough for your mom's scarf!"

"But I can't keep it! Bill said he'd only get the job if he didn't make mistakes this week."

"It's only a dollar," Sara argued. "He won't know who he gave it to, and they won't fire him for it. They'll think it was the machine's fault."

For a second Jayne hesitated. It would be nice to buy the scarf today, but she thought of Bill. She thought of how it would feel to be on a real job. She would want anyone who got too much change to give it back.

Then that's what I have to do, Jayne thought. *Even if I didn't know Bill, I'd have to do it.*

Jayne expected Sara to laugh or be angry when she told her, but instead Sara nodded. "I know. It's really hard to do what's right sometimes, though. I'll go back with you. But what about your mother's scarf?"

"I'll ask dad to *lend* me the money," Jayne said. "I'll pay him back, and then the scarf will be all from me—honestly."

Action Idea: Keep thinking about this verse, the Golden Rule. The next time you must decide how to act with someone, think carefully about how you would feel if you were in their place and they were in yours. Then decide what to do. You may surprise that person. Then you can tell them about the Golden Rule.

I wish I could have been there when you were preaching, Jesus. I would like to have heard what you said. I would like to have asked you questions. But I can read what you said in the Bible. Help me to remember what you said and did. Help me to treat everyone the way I would like them to treat me.

6 Branch Out!

As Jesus was getting into the boat, the man who had been demon-possessed begged to go with him. But Jesus did not let him, but said, "Go home to your family and tell them how much the Lord has done for you, and how he has had mercy on you."

Mark 5:18-19
(Read from the beginning of the chapter to get the whole story.)

Jesus and his disciples had rowed their boat across the lake. Now they were in a lonely place where people buried the dead. A man who was not always in his right mind lived there. The people of his town had tried to keep him chained at home, but he was too strong. He broke the chains. His family

35

and friends made him live alone in the cemetery because they were afraid he would hurt someone when he was not sane.

The Bible does not tell us what this man looked like, but we can imagine. He must have been very big, with powerful arms, to be able to break chains. He was probably dirty. His hair very likely was long and matted because he did not comb it. He did not wear many clothes. If you had seen him wandering among the graves, you would probably have been frightened too. You would have wanted to run away.

This man recognized Jesus as God's Son. He knew he had done bad things when he was not in his right mind. He was afraid Jesus would hurt him. Instead, Jesus loved him and healed him.

Naturally the man was very grateful to Jesus. He asked Jesus to let him go with the disciples. But Jesus would not do that. He had a special job for this man. He told him to go home to his family and tell everyone what Jesus had done for him.

The man may have been disappointed. It may have seemed more important to him to go with Jesus. But he did what Jesus told him to. When he told his friends about Jesus, they were filled with wonder.

Today Jesus needs people to go all over the world as missionaries. But he also needs people to stay home and tell their friends about him. You do not have to be rich or important to tell your friends about Jesus. You don't even have to be a grown-up!

The moving van had left the house next door when Carol knocked at the back door.

36

"I'm Carol Waverly," she told the woman who answered. "We live next door. Mom sent over some cookies. I saw a girl outside. Can she come over to play?"

The woman smiled. "Our name is Fitch, and Janice is my daughter."

Just then a girl about Carol's age came to the door. "Hi," she said. She grinned at Carol.

The girls soon found they had a lot in common. They both liked to read and to ride their bicycles. They both liked to play games and watch TV. They played together the rest of the day.

The next day was Saturday. Carol and Janice went to the library in the morning. In the afternoon they rode their bicycles downtown so Carol could show Janice where everything was.

"Let's go to the park tomorrow morning," Janice said when the girls separated that night. "The playground looks like a lot of fun."

"I can't go 'til afternoon," Carol said. "I go to Sunday school and church in the morning."

Janice looked surprised. "No kidding? What do you do there? Is it fun?"

Carol suddenly got an idea. "You're new, so why don't you come with me? We have a neat class, and you'll like our teacher. We do fun things, and we learn about Jesus too. Then we all sit together in church. Our pastor's great too. Mostly he talks so we can understand it."

Janice looked thoughtful. "We've moved a lot, so I haven't gone to Sunday school much. But I

37

think I'd like to go with you. In all the places we've lived, you're the first person who ever invited me! What time should I be ready?"

Action Idea: Who do you know who doesn't go to Sunday school? Invite that person to go with you next Sunday. Offer to pick her up at her house. Make sure you and the others in your class make her feel welcome, and ask her to come back next week. Help her with the lesson.

It's hard for me to believe that some people don't know much about you, Jesus. Help me to be a friend to these people. Help me to show them how much you love them by inviting them to Sunday school and church. Thank you for the people who teach our Sunday school classes, and for our pastor.

7 What Do You Say, Lord?

One day Jesus was praying in a certain place. When he finished, one of his disciples said to him, "Lord, teach us to pray, just as John taught his disciples."
Luke 11:1

Jesus prayed often. Sometimes he prayed where his disciples could see him, but often he went away alone to pray as well. The disciples had seen how praying made Jesus feel close to God. They wanted to feel that close to God too.

Jesus taught the disciples the Lord's Prayer. Jesus did not mean for them to pray only that prayer. He wanted his followers to talk to God as they would talk to a friend walking beside them. He wanted his people to know that praying was as easy as speaking their thoughts.

Jesus said other things about prayer. He did not want us to pray to get special attention from other people. He told us to go off alone to pray.

Jesus did not mean we should not pray out loud with others in Sunday school, church, and family devotions. He meant we should not be thinking so much about how we sound to other people that we forget we are talking to God.

When you pray, don't worry about the right words, the right place, or the right time. God understands your thoughts as well as your words. Talk to him as though he were your best friend.

Sometimes people say, "I prayed and prayed, but God didn't answer my prayers!" The apostle Paul wrote in 2 Corinthians 12:8-9 that he had prayed three times for Christ to take away a "thorn in my flesh." No one knows exactly what that "thorn" was, but God did not take it away. Instead he promised Paul, "My grace is sufficient for you."

God always answers our prayers! Sometimes he says "Yes." Other times he says "No," as he did to Paul—and then gave him something even better than he had asked for! God also says "Wait a while" or "not yet" to answer our prayers. We are always in a hurry, but God knows the best time for everything.

So if God's answer to your prayers seems to be no, remember God is still with you, helping you with his strength and love.

Judy's grandmother was very sick. She had been sick a long time. She could not be out of bed, and she was in the hospital often. Even at home she had to take many kinds of medicine and shots. Judy prayed every night that God would make her grandmother better.

One day Judy's grandmother died. Judy cried and cried.

"Why did God let grandma die?" Judy asked her mother. "I prayed and asked him to make her better! Now I'll never see her again! Why?"

Judy's mother put her arms around her. "You were praying God would make grandma the way she was two years ago before she got sick, weren't you?"

"Sure." Judy thought that was a silly question. What else could getting better mean?

"You wanted grandma to be out of the hospital and feel good and not have to take any more medicine?" Judy's mother asked.

"Sure!" *This was getting sillier and sillier*, Judy thought. What was wrong with her mother?

"Then God did answer your prayers, Judy! Think about it. Grandma isn't in the hospital any more. She doesn't have to take any more medicine. And she doesn't have any more pain! Someday we know we'll see her again in heaven. Do you think she would want you to be sad about that?"

Judy thought it over. She would have liked God to make grandma healthy, but her mother's mother was an old woman and she had been very sick.

"I guess God did answer my prayers," Judy admitted slowly. "It wasn't exactly the way I wanted him to, but I'm going to thank him for making it so grandma doesn't ever have to be sick again."

Action Idea: During your prayer time this week make a list of the things you ask of God. Next to each thing, write down how God answers that prayer. Remember, though, that many times God says "Wait" when we want a quick answer. Remember, too, that prayer is not just asking God to do things. Prayer is also thanking God for what he has done for us and worshiping him as the only God.

Lord, I know that sometimes I pray for things that are not right for me and for others. I am glad you don't always answer our prayers the way we think you should. I am glad you always answer us though. Help me to see the way you answer my prayers, even when it isn't right away or the way I thought you would answer. Help me to see that "No" and "Wait a while" are answers to prayer too. Thank you for listening to all our prayers.

8 Me? Love Her? Are You Kidding?

*On the contrary: "If your enemy is hungry, feed him;
if he is thirsty, give him something to drink. In doing
this, you will heap burning coals on his head." Do
not be overcome by evil, but overcome evil with
good.*

Romans 12:20-21

Paul wrote these verses to Christians living in the
great city of Rome. You can read them, too, in Proverbs 25:21-22. The Roman empire was the most
powerful in the world in those days. Its armies had
conquered most of the world, and the city of Rome
was its capital.

Rome was a big city; more than one million people
lived there. Foreigners came to Rome on business.

If you had walked along the streets of Rome you would have seen people in many different kinds of clothes. You would have heard many different languages being spoken.

Unfortunately, Rome was an evil city. The government, headed by the emperor, was corrupt. Many evil things went on all over the city. Yet there were also Christians there.

These Roman Christians did not have an easy time. It was dangerous to be a Christian then, and it would have been easy for the Christians to hate the Romans who persecuted them. But Paul wrote to tell the Christians in Rome how they must act as people of God.

Followers of Jesus were not to hate their enemies; they were to love them! Jesus had told them that. He had shown them his love when he died on the cross and when he forgave the men who had put him there.

Now Paul was showing the Christians some practical ways to show their love for their enemies. They were to help them, even if they had to share their food with them!

Paul told the people that by helping their enemy they would "heap burning coals upon his head." Paul did not mean there would be real burning coals, of course. That would not be loving or helping an enemy!

Paul meant that by being kind to an enemy, it would make that person feel badly that he had done wrong or been mean to someone who was being good to him. He would be sorry for the way he had treated the Christian. Then, Paul said, the Christian would be the winner because good would win over evil. The old enemy would be a friend instead.

When Sue got to the park pool for her swimming lesson, she was glad to see that Karen Bowles was not there. Karen was the meanest girl Sue knew. She was always pushing people so they would fall into the water. She had teased Sue because Sue had been afraid of the water when the lessons had started. Karen had gotten the others to laugh at Sue too. Sue had been embarrassed, angry, and hurt—all at once.

At least I'm not afraid of the water now, Sue thought. *I wonder where Karen is.*

The instructor answered that question as soon as everyone was there.

"Karen Bowles will not be here for any more lessons," the instructor said. "She was hit by a car last night while she was on her bike. She's at home, but she'll be in bed and have a cast on her leg for several weeks."

"Then she can't toss us in the water!" the girl next to Sue whispered. "I'm glad she won't be here!"

Sue started to agree, but she stopped. No one liked Karen because of the way she treated everyone, but being in bed when you weren't really sick couldn't be much fun. Karen would be bored with no one to play with.

46

Later, when Sue was going home, she remembered the Bible verses she had read a few evenings before. They were about loving and helping your enemies.

But I can't love her! Sue thought. *Karen's too mean!* Then she sighed. Jesus had loved the ones who put him on the cross, and that was pretty mean!

But Karen isn't hungry or thirsty, Sue thought. Then she had an idea. *I'll go see her! I'll take her a book!*

When Sue entered Karen's room, Karen looked at her suspiciously. "What are you doing here?" she asked.

"I came to see you," Sue said. "I brought you a book, and I thought you might like someone to play games with."

Karen was quiet for a minute. "Yeah, I'd like to play Monopoly. TV's boring, and I get tired of reading all the time. But how come you're doing this? You're not my friend! I mean, I pushed you into the pool—"

"We haven't been friends," Sue admitted. "But we could be. That's why I came."

"We'll see," Karen said. "Get out the game."

As Sue set up the Monopoly game, she smiled to herself. She felt better inside about Karen than she ever had before.

Action Idea: Think of one person who has treated you badly or unfairly. Think of one nice thing you could do for that person. Do it. It could be helping a younger brother or sister with homework, or visiting someone who is sick, like Sue did.

It's easy for me to love my friends, Lord. They are nice to me. It is easy to do nice things for them in return. I don't have any real enemies, like in a war, Lord. But there are a few people who have been mean to me. Help me to think of a way to be kind to them. And thank you for all my friends, Lord.

9　Make Her Help Me!

But Martha was distracted by all the preparations that had to be made. She came to him and asked, "Lord, don't you care that my sister has left me to do the work by myself? Tell her to help me!"

Luke 10:40

Jesus was visiting in the home of Martha, her sister Mary, and her brother Lazarus. They lived in Bethany, just a few miles east of Jerusalem. Jesus often stayed there when he was on his way to or from Jerusalem. Lazarus was the man Jesus raised from the dead shortly before Jesus himself died on the cross.

Mary and Martha were like many sisters—they were very different from each other. We do not know if they were different in their looks, but we know from the Bible that they were very different in personality. They were different in what they thought was important.

Martha was in charge of the house. She wanted everything to run smoothly. She wanted the house to be clean and neat when guests came. She wanted a hearty meal to be served to them, hot and on time. She wanted everything in the house to be perfect. She was willing to work hard all day to make sure everything in the house was just right.

Mary was more interested in listening to the men talk and exchange ideas. She especially liked to listen when Jesus talked. She thought this was more important than getting a big meal ready on time. Mary would have been willing to eat a cold snack if she could keep listening to Jesus.

When Martha asked Jesus to tell Mary to help her with the housework, Jesus did not. He reminded Martha that what Mary was doing at that time was more important, in the long run, than what Martha was doing.

Jesus did not mean that he did not appreciate everything Martha had done. He did not mean he did not like a clean house or enjoy a good meal. Jesus simply wanted Martha to recognize what was most important at that particular time.

Perhaps Jesus spoke privately to Mary later and suggested she help Martha more in the house. The sisters would never be exactly alike, but each could learn to understand and appreciate what the other felt. Jesus loved both sisters. He wanted to see them love each other too.

Aubry was angry. It was Saturday morning, the time when she and her sister, Katie, were to clean the bedroom they shared.

"Mom!" Aubry wailed. "Make Katie help me!"

"I have to go to church to practice my solo for tomorrow," Katie argued.

"It's because you're four years older!" Aubry said. "It would be different if I was oldest!"

"Can't you clean your room together this afternoon?" their mother asked.

Katie shook her head. "We have our youth hike and picnic. I have to go on that."

"Well, I'm not doing it all myself!" Aubry stamped back to the bedroom. "Katie has all the fun while I do all the work! I know! I'll only clean my half! That'll show Katie!"

Aubry straightened her half of the wide desk the girls shared. She changed the sheets on her bed. She dusted her part of the bookshelves and her own dresser. She vacuumed the carpet only on her side of the room.

Aubry looked at the room. Her half was clean, but something was wrong.

Katie's messy side makes the whole room look messy! Aubry thought. *Now what should I do?*

For a minute Aubry wanted to run out and shut the door. But that would mean she had wasted her time cleaning. If Aubry wanted her side to look good, she would have to clean Katie's side too!

Aubry worked as fast as she could until the whole room was done.

"Aubry!" Katie came running in just as Aubry finished. She stopped. "You cleaned it! All alone! Thank you!" Katie hugged Aubry. "I have a surprise too! We can take guests on the hike, so I said I was taking you! We'll hike, and then there'll be the campfire—"

Aubry looked at her sister in surprise. "But you didn't know I was cleaning the whole room! Why did you say you'd bring me on the hike?"

Katie gave Aubry another quick hug. "Why, because we're sisters, silly!"

Action Idea: Do an extra chore for a brother or sister. You might do dishes, pick up toys, or make a bed for them. Tell them you are doing it because you love them and Jesus. Plan your chore time so you still have time to read your Bible and pray too. Be a Martha *and* a Mary for Jesus.

I don't know if I'm a Martha or a Mary, Lord. I wish I could have cooked a dinner for you to eat. I wish I could have listened to you talk and tell stories too. Help me to be both a Martha and a Mary—for you and for my family. Help me not to get angry with my brothers or sisters or parents when I think I am doing more than my share of the work. Thank you for Mary and Martha.

10   Playing by the Rules

Submit yourselves for the Lord's sake to every authority instituted among men.

1 Peter 2:13

Peter had been the chief disciple with Jesus. Now that Jesus had gone back to God, Peter was in charge of the church on earth.

When Peter wrote this letter, the government of Rome was an evil one. The Roman empire was corrupt and crumbling. In a few years the wicked, cruel emperor, Nero, would blame the Christians for causing the great fire that burned much of the city of Rome. Nero would have many Christians killed by lions in the arena and in other horrible ways.

The Christians knew that the government of Rome was evil. They did not want to obey unfair laws. They did not want to obey an emperor who thought he was a god. They knew there was only one God and that Jesus was his Son.

But Peter said they must submit to, or obey, *every* authority set up by men. The Christians were to do this, not only for their own personal safety, but "for the Lord's sake." They were to obey the laws so that unbelievers could not look at Christians and say they broke laws or were troublemakers. Peter knew behavior like that would not help the Lord's kingdom to grow.

Peter wanted the Christians to be good examples to their unbelieving neighbors. By obeying the laws and submitting to authority, they would make the Lord's name respected, even by people who did not believe Jesus was the Son of God.

Today it is not dangerous for us to be Christians because we live in a free country. Still, there are many rules and authorities we do not want to obey. A rule seems silly, or it doesn't seem to apply to us. We see no harm in breaking it—at least just this once.

But Peter tells us we must obey the leaders who have been elected or appointed over us. We are to respect them and follow the rules so no one will be able to say Christians are not good citizens.

The traffic light turned red as Margie reached the curb. There were no cars coming, so she dashed across the street anyway. A sharp whistle blast stopped her.

"Oh, hi, Dave." Margie was relieved. The crossing guard was her favorite cousin.

"You crossed against the light!" Dave accused. "That means a ticket!"

Margie's eyes opened wide. "You can't do that! I'll have to go to the school office and maybe get detention! You're my cousin!"

"It's the school rule. I have to make sure everyone follows it." Dave did not sound happy. He handed the ticket to Margie.

"There weren't any cars coming!" Margie grabbed the ticket and marched off. Dave was mean! Angrily she tore the ticket to shreds.

Just before noon, Margie's teacher asked for someone to help with the first graders on the playground after lunch. Margie raised her hand. She liked watching the smaller children.

Margie was at the far end of the playground, away from the teacher, when she saw four girls walking backward up the slide. She ran over.

"You're not allowed—"

"Hi, Margie." It was Margie's little sister, Sharon. "Don't worry," Sharon told her friends. "This is my big sister. She won't care if we don't follow that dumb rule!"

"It may be dumb, but it's a rule," Margie said firmly. "You have to follow it, even if I am your sister! Or I'll have to call the teacher!"

"Oh, all right!" Sharon and her friends stomped off angrily.

Margie stared after them in surprise. "She thought I'd let them do it just because she's my sister!" Suddenly Margie remembered that morning. Dave had done his duty too, and she had been angry with him.

That's different, Margie thought. But she knew it wasn't. Dave had been right then, and she had been right now.

Margie started across the playground. She didn't want to go to the office, but she had broken a rule. She would find the ticket she had torn up. Then she would apologize to Dave.

Action Idea: Think of the rule you find hardest to follow in school. Do the same for the rules at home and in church. Ask yourself what would happen if everyone suddenly stopped obeying these rules. It may help you to write this down in your notebook. For a week, try to obey all these rules. Then ask yourself if following these rules made you a better citizen and Christian this week.

I don't like having to follow so many rules, Lord. Some are silly, and I don't see any reason to even have them! But I know you want your people to obey the rules and the people in charge. So please help me to do it for you and to be a good example of how a Christian should live. Thank you for givinq us parents, teachers, church leaders, and other authorities who teach us and help us grow up to be good citizens and Christians.

11 Oh, Mother!

Children, obey your parents in everything, for this pleases the Lord.

Colossians 3:20

The Bible has many kinds of information and instruction in it. Much of the Bible tells us about God and our relationship with him. But there is also instruction on how we must live with other people, especially within our own family.

We don't know much about Jesus when he was a child. We know about his birth and escape to Egypt. We know when his parents brought him back to Nazareth. We read of his being in the Temple when he was only 12, arguing with the smartest people of his day. Luke (2:51-52) tells us that when Jesus went back to Nazareth with his parents after that trip to

Jerusalem, he "was obedient to them." And Jesus "grew in wisdom and stature, and in favor with God and men."

Jesus obeyed his parents, and Paul says children must obey "in everything." Paul did not say you are to obey your parents only when you want to, or only when you think they are right, or only when your folks are around to punish you if you don't obey. Paul said children were to obey "in everything."

Paul went on to tell the children why they must obey their parents. It is not to make your parents happy or to keep peace in the family, although it will do both. But you are to obey your parents because "this pleases the Lord."

Have you ever thought that not doing what your parents told you was a way of upsetting Jesus? Or that obeying your parents was making Jesus happy?

It is not always fun to obey your parents. But Paul leaves no way out except to obey "in everything."

Why do you do what your parents tell you? You should not be doing it out of fear, or even because you respect their judgment. You should obey out of love for them and for God.

When school was let out early because of a bad snowstorm, Lynn asked Cathy to come over to her house.

"I'm not supposed to go anywhere if I didn't ask before," Cathy said. "And I can't call mom at work unless it's a real big emergency."

"You didn't know this morning it would snow so hard," Lynn argued. "My mom's at work too, and we have a new video game."

Cathy thought about playing the new game. "OK. I'll leave for home at 3:30, the time when school would usually be out."

The girls had been playing the new game a long time when the screen suddenly went dark.

"The lights are out!" Cathy scrambled to her feet. "I'd better go home!"

The girls looked out the window. It had snowed a lot more; there were drifts everywhere.

"I'd better call mom and tell her to come get me," Cathy decided.

But when Cathy picked up the telephone, it was dead.

"Lynn, I can't call mom, and I'm scared to walk home in the storm!"

"Wait," Lynn advised. "The phone'll be fixed soon."

At four o'clock the telephone was still not working. Cathy picked up her books. "I'm going home! Mom will be there soon, and she'll worry! Maybe I can get a ride if a policeman or someone I know comes along."

Cathy pulled on her cap. She was praying Jesus would help her get home safely. It was cold as she started slowly along the edge of the street. Then a car came along, stopped, and someone called Cathy's name.

"Mom!" Cathy flung herself into her mother's arms. "How did you know to come here? I didn't know if I could get home, and I was scared."

In the warm car, Cathy's mother explained. "I called home. When you didn't answer, I began to worry. I tried calling every 10 minutes. When the phone went out, I decided to check at Lynn's."

"Oh, mom, I'm so glad you did! I was worried about you being worried—" Cathy blew her nose hard. "I'm sorry I broke the rule. I'm sorry you worried and had to come for me. But I know better now; I won't ever do it again!"

Action Idea: If there is a rule in your family that you feel is unfair, ask your parents to set a time when you can all talk about it. Make it a time when none of you is tired, hungry, or upset about anything else. Present your arguments in a quiet voice. If your parents still do not feel the rule should be changed, accept their judgment, "for this pleases the Lord."

Sometimes I don't want to do what my parents say, Lord. I think they try to run my life too much. They act like I'm still a baby! I want to run my own life. But I want to please you, too, Jesus. Help me to obey my parents "in everything" the way You obeyed Mary and Joseph. I want to grow in wisdom and stature and in favor with you and the people around me.

12   Need A Hand?

Carry each other's burdens, and in this way you will fulfill the law of Christ.

Galatians 6:2

The apostle Paul was telling the Christians living in Galatia how Jesus wanted them to live with each other. The things Paul told them were not only for the Galatians, though. Paul's advice was for all Christians then, and even today.

You know that when you have a heavy package or bundle it's a lot easier to carry if someone helps you. You are grateful to that person for helping, and you feel good toward her from then on. You look for ways to help the one who helped you.

Carrying heavy packages for other people is a good thing to do. But Paul did not mean that was the

only way Christians were to help others. Paul meant much more by his words; he called all the problems people have "burdens."

Paul reminds us that Jesus wants us to help each other. We should be looking for ways to help our fellow Christians live with and solve their problems, no matter what those problems are. Then we will be obeying Christ's law.

Christians have the same problems as other people. Sometimes helping may be as simple as carrying a heavy package. Other times the problems are more serious. People are often lonely or poor. Someone might be behind in his schoolwork because he has been sick.

How can Christians help carry each other's burdens? You may think that because you are not an adult yet that you can't do much to help others. But you can pray for those you know have problems. You can refuse to gossip about other people and their burdens. You can ask your pastor or parents what else you can do to help a specific person. Perhaps you can mow the lawn for someone who is sick or read to someone who is lonely.

Carrying someone else's burdens will help that person. But it will also help you because it will make you feel glad that you have done what Jesus wants you to do.

Robyn was feeding Lightning, her new dog, when her mother called her to help carry the groceries next door to Mrs. O'Hara. When she did her own shopping, Robyn's mother bought the old woman's groceries too.

Mrs. O'Hara held the screen door open with her cane. "Thank you so much! I don't know what I'd do without neighbors like you."

"I got a dog!" Robyn said. "Dad says it isn't just one kind; it's lots of kinds!"

"Wonderful!" Mrs. O'Hara smiled. "We had a dog. He was so much company after my husband died— But I couldn't take care of one now."

That night Lightning lay on the floor beside Robyn's bed. Robyn could touch his silky head just by reaching out her hand. It was nice to have Lightning to talk to after she had said her prayers and read her Bible.

"I bet Mrs. O'Hara misses her dog," Robyn told Lightning. "She doesn't have anyone to talk to all day except if someone comes to see her." Robyn tried to imagine how it would feel to be alone all day. She decided it would be awful! She wanted her family and friends to talk to and laugh with and do things with. Robyn wanted Lightning to talk to when no one else was around.

Then Robyn got an idea. The next morning her parents agreed she could ask Mrs. O'Hara.

Robyn and Lightning went to see Mrs. O'Hara. Mrs. O'Hara held Lightning and petted him. He licked her face. They were friends right away.

"Mrs. O'Hara, would you like to have Lightning?" Robyn asked. "Not all the time, though. I'd bring him in the morning before school and take him home at night. You wouldn't have to take

64

care of him. I'd feed him and everything. He wouldn't be any trouble for you."

Mrs. O'Hara smiled, and Robyn thought she saw tears in the old woman's eyes.

"Oh, I'd like that! " said Mrs. O'Hara. "Thank you, Robyn. Lightning will keep me from being lonely. And every time we play, I'll think of how nice you are to share Lightning with me."

Action Idea: Help someone this week. It could be a young mother who needs a free baby-sitter. It could be a friend who needs extra help with schoolwork. It could be a younger brother or sister who needs help cleaning his or her room. If you cannot think of anyone, ask your parents or pastor to suggest someone.

I'm not sure I know anyone with a "burden" that I can help carry, Lord. If there is someone, would you please help me to find that person? I want to do things to help others, like Paul says you want us to do. Show me what to do, Lord, and when to do it. Thank you for people like Paul who taught us how to live like you want us to.

13 You Can Do It!

*Each of us should please his neighbor for his good,
to build him up.*

Romans 15:2

Building each other up, or encouraging each other,
is one way Christians can help each other. Everyone
needs to hear the words "You can do it!" often. There
are many times when we feel we cannot do what we
know we must try. So, Paul says, Christians must
build up their neighbors.

"Building up" means exactly the opposite of "tearing down." Some people seem to enjoy tearing down
their neighbors, family, and friends; they spend so
much time doing it! They tear down other people by
saying things like, "You'd better not try that. You can't
do it." Or "You don't have the ability to do that. Let

someone with more talent do it." Or "I knew you'd mess that up!"

People who tear down often use words like *dumb*, *clumsy*, and *silly* when they are talking about other people. Tearing down is *not* what a Christian should do, Paul says.

Building up or encouraging means more than giving a friend a "high five" when she does something super. Building up means standing by your friend even when things go wrong. It means making her feel good that she tried something new and hard, even if it didn't turn out exactly the way she wanted. Building up means reassuring her that failing in something today does not mean she will fail in what she tries tomorrow. Building up means reminding your friend that Jesus is with her, and that he understands the problems and that things will get better.

In the fourth verse of this part of his letter to Roman Christians, Paul reminds us that we are to be encouraged through the Scriptures. Paul assumed that Christians would study God's Word and know it. You can be encouraged yourself and encourage others only if you know what the Bible promises and teaches.

When Betsy got to the bus stop, Ginny Adams and two of her friends were there. So was Greg Cummings. Greg was mentally retarded. He and his family went to Betsy's church.

"Today I'm going to work all by myself," Greg said proudly.

68

"That's great!" It was hard for Betsy to imagine a big person like Greg never riding a bus alone before.

Ginny and her friends laughed and moved away.

Betsy looked at Greg. Why did they have to laugh at him? Greg was cheerful and kind, and it wasn't his fault he wasn't very smart.

Ginny and her friends came back. "Which bus is yours, Greg?" they asked.

Greg pulled a paper from his pocket. "The one with a sign like this."

"Not today," said Ginny, winking at her friends. "Today you take the one coming now."

Greg frowned as he studied the sign on the bus. "No," he said slowly.

"Yes!" Ginny insisted. "Hurry or you'll be late for work!"

Greg looked confused, and Betsy did not know what to do. If she told Greg the others were playing a trick, they would be angry at her. Surely someone would get Greg on the right bus, even if he took the wrong one now. *But Greg will be scared and late for work*, she thought.

Greg was starting for the bus. Betsy grabbed his arm. "You're right, Greg. It's not your bus. They were just teasing."

Greg came back slowly. Ginny and the others had disappeared. "I can't tell my bus very good," Greg mumbled. "Why did they do that?"

"They were teasing," Betsy repeated. "But you *can* tell which bus is yours, Greg! Just show your paper to the driver. He'll tell you if it's the wrong bus! You can go by yourself!"

Greg suddenly grinned. "Sure I can! Mom and dad and you and the man at work say I can! Now I say it too!"

"Here's your bus." Betsy pointed. "Go on, Greg, and tell everyone you came to work by yourself on the right bus!"

Action Idea: Tomorrow keep track of how often you tear someone down. Did you call your little sister "stupid"? Did you tell a friend that he's too clumsy to play ball? The day after tomorrow, keep track of how often you encourage someone. Can you help your little sister with her homework so she understands it better? Can you show your friend how to swing a bat better? Just saying "You can do it!" helps encourage people around you.

I don't know why it's easier to tear people down than to build them up, Lord. I don't want to hurt anyone by making them feel they can't do something. I want to help them instead. But so many times I say the wrong thing. Please help me to think about what I say before I say it so that my words will build up and encourage, not tear down and discourage. And thank you for your constant encouragement to me.

14 A Little Responsibility

Whoever can be trusted with very little can also be trusted with much, and whoever is dishonest with very little will also be dishonest with much.

Luke 16:10

Have you ever told yourself that what you do today doesn't really make much difference to your future? After all, you're not even in high school yet, let alone graduated. Have you ever wondered if how you spend your time and money now, how well you do your homework, and how often you clean your room could possibly have anything to do with the kind of woman you will be some day? In this verse, Jesus says it has everything to do with how you will act and the kind of person you will be in the future.

Jesus says that the servant who does well when she is trusted with only a little responsibility will do well when she is promoted and given more important work to do. The opposite is true too, Jesus says. The person who does not do her job well when it does not seem important will not do it well if she ever gets the chance to do something bigger.

Right now you are like the servant who is being given only a little responsibility. Your "job" right now is to grow strong—in your body, in your mind, and in your relationship to Jesus. If you do a good job at this, you will be ready for more and bigger responsibilities when you are a woman.

Habits we develop when we are young tend to stick with us through life unless we make a serious effort to change them. Getting into bad habits is simple at any age. Getting out of them is hard, and the longer you have had that bad habit, the harder it is to change it.

Jesus says that when you are young you must learn to be trustworthy and responsible with what you have been given. Then you will be ready for more and bigger opportunities when you are grown. Everything you do now will influence the kind of Christian woman you will be in a few years.

The screen flashed "Game Over," and Leigh sighed. That had been her last token. The only money she had left were the two dollar bills she had saved to give to help redecorate the nursery department at Sunday school.

Leigh watched the others playing the video games. Her fingers ached to play again. Leigh thought of the Sunday school money.

I can put it back when I get my allowance to-morrow, Leigh thought.

Leigh bought more tokens with one of the dollar bills, but in a few minutes they were gone.

"You were really close to a new record," someone said. "Bet you could do it next time!"

"I know I can!" Leigh put down her last dollar for tokens. It was easier this time.

On her third game, Leigh broke the machine record. Everyone cheered, and she felt like a heroine.

When Leigh got her allowance the next day, she put two dollars aside. It did not leave much money for the whole week.

"Dad, I—could I borrow some extra?" Leigh asked.

"Those arcade games again?" Her father sounded disappointed. "Leigh, you were late getting home yesterday. Your mother had to do your job and set the table. Now you need more money—"

"I set a machine record!" Leigh retorted, but it didn't sound as important now.

"Video games are fine," her father said, "if you don't let them become the most important thing in your life! But you've done that. I'm sorry, but if you can't handle the responsibility for your own money and time, I'll have to limit what you can spend at the arcade."

Leigh looked down at the floor. Her father was right; she had spent too much time and money on the games. She had not been a very responsible person.

Leigh nodded. "OK, dad. Maybe if you help me, I can learn to play them without forgetting everything else."

Action Idea: Choose one bad habit you want to break. Think of ways you can change it. You may have to change your activities. You may have to change your daily schedule. Try not to give in to this habit for three weeks. Ask your family to help you. Ask God to help you too.

I know I have some bad habits, Lord. I really do want to be a person who can be trusted in little things so that I can grow up to be the kind of woman you want me to be. I want to be a woman who can be trusted to do a good job in the important things of my life. Help me to break my bad habits. Remind me each time I give in and show me how to be the kind of person you want me to be right now.

15   Whose Side Are You On?

*No one can serve two masters. Either he will hate
the one and love the other, or he will be devoted to
the one and despise the other. You cannot serve
both God and Money.*

Matthew 6:24

This verse is only a small part of Jesus' most famous sermon: the Sermon on the Mount. The whole
sermon is Chapters 5, 6, and 7 of Matthew.

The people who had come out to hear Jesus that
day knew about servants. Most families in those days
had at least one servant. If a person was not rich
enough to have a servant, they or their families were
probably servants themselves. Everyone knew what
Jesus meant when he said no one could serve two
masters equally.

Who would want a servant who tried to serve someone else too? Each master would be afraid the other master was getting the best work from the servant because the servant loved the other master more.

If a servant tried to serve two masters, she would not be able to answer the call of one while working for the other. It wouldn't matter how badly she was needed. There would be no one to do her work for one master while she was busy serving the other.

Jesus said we cannot serve both God and Money. Jesus talked about money many times in the New Testament. Jesus knew people had to have money to live. He knew they had to work to earn money for food, clothes, and shelter. Jesus meant that his people should not want to earn a lot of money so badly that they forgot to serve and worship God and to put God first in their lives.

Paul warned Timothy (1 Timothy 6:10) that the love of money was a root, or start, of all kinds of evil. God gave each of us talents and abilities. How we use these is our choice. We can use the gifts God gave us to honor him, or we can use them to get money and worldly praise. God does not force us to serve him, but he does ask, "Whose side are you on?"

Dena was the best artist in her school. She wanted to be a painter when she was through school, or maybe draw pictures for children's books.

One day Dena's older brother brought a friend home. When Bruce saw Dena's pictures on the wall, he was impressed.

"These are good!" Bruce said. "Would you draw a big picture for me to put on the door of my dorm room at college? I'd pay you."

"Pay me?" Dena was excited. She had never gotten paid for drawing before! "Sure! I'll draw a dog, or—"

Bruce laughed. "No. I know what I want." He pulled a sheet of paper from his pocket. It was a picture cut from a magazine. "Can you draw this, Dena?"

Dena looked at the picture. She felt her face getting hot. It was a picture of a woman with hardly any clothes on. Dena had seen pictures like this before, but she had never thought of drawing one!

"You're good enough to do it for me," Bruce encouraged her.

Dena hesitated. She knew she could draw the picture. She could draw almost anything, especially if she had something to copy from. But this did not seem like the kind of picture she should draw. "It's—it's not what I want to draw," Dena said slowly. "I could do something else for you—"

Bruce put the picture back in his pocket. "This is what I want, but I should have known a kid like you couldn't handle it. I'll find someone else."

Dena watched as Bruce left. She wondered if she should feel sad at losing her first chance to earn money by drawing, but she didn't. She felt good inside.

Action Idea: Choose your best talent. Think of ways you could use it to serve God. Write down all the ways in your notebook. Choose one way and try to find a chance to use your talent for God that way this week.

Thank you for giving me special talents, Lord. Help me to develop them until they are the very best they can be. Help me to serve only one master with them—you. Show me ways I can use my talents to serve you now, Lord, and not just some day when I'm grown up. I can't always see the chances my-self, so I need you to point them out to me and to help me do what I should.

16 Watch Your Language!

But now you must rid yourselves of all such things as these: anger, rage, malice, slander, and filthy language from your lips.

Colossians 3:8

Once again Paul was trying to help Christians learn how to live lives pleasing to God. The first sins he mentioned sound serious: anger, rage, malice, and slander. But the last one, filthy language, doesn't seem bad enough to be listed with the others. It is to God, though!

You live in a time when filthy language is everywhere. Sometimes it's called "street talk" to make it seem more acceptable. Sometimes it's referred to as "four-letter words" because that's the length of many of these words. Sometimes filthy language is using the name of God or Jesus in a disrespectful way.

You hear filthy language every day on TV, on the playground—almost everywhere. You also read it. Four-letter words and God's name appear in books and magazines. They show up on the walls of rest rooms and deserted buildings. It is hard to get away from filthy language.

The early Christians lived in a world of such language too, even though it was a different tongue than you speak. Paul knew the danger to Christians when they heard this kind of talk over and over. First, the mind begins to accept it as normal, as the "all right" thing. The next step is to slip into using it.

You may not use God's name the wrong way yourself, but have you lost your surprise when others do? You may not use four-letter words when you are angry, but do you almost expect them from others? You may have come to think this kind of talk can't be so bad if so many people use it.

God does not want his people to use language that is not helpful to themselves and others. He wants his name spoken only with reverence. Watching your language means more than being careful of what you say. It also means checking what you see on TV and read in books. You cannot always avoid the filthy language others use, but you can be alert to keep it from your own lips, as Paul instructed.

Amy was spending the night with Connie. Connie's parents had gone to visit a sick friend.

"Come see what my brother forgot when he went back to college last weekend!" Connie told Amy.

Connie lifted the mattress on her bed and pulled out a paperback book. "Read this!" She put her finger on a paragraph.

The words seemed to leap from the page. Amy knew she was blushing. "Connie, we shouldn't be reading this!"

"Oh, come on!"

"But these words—"

Connie shrugged. "That's how people talk." She shoved the book back under the mattress. "Let's watch TV. With mom and dad gone, we can watch whatever we want."

Connie turned on a program Amy's parents did not allow her to watch at home. Amy squirmed as she watched and listened. The people used God's and Jesus' names a lot, but not in the right way. They used other bad language too. But Connie was laughing, so Amy laughed too. *It couldn't hurt to watch just this once*, she thought.

Later, as the girls got ready for bed, Connie dropped her toothbrush. "Oh, __ __ __ __!" she said, using one of the words the people on TV had used.

"Connie!" Amy had never heard her friend talk like that.

Connie giggled. "Sorry. Guess I watched too much TV."

In bed, Amy thought about the evening. Connie had said reading that book and watching that TV show wouldn't hurt, but she ended up using one of those words herself. *I wonder if she'll do it again?* Amy thought. She rolled over, still thinking. *And if reading that book isn't wrong, why does she hide it? And she turned off the TV when she heard her folks coming! If it was all right, we should be able to let everyone know about it! Maybe we forgot that tonight. But I'm going to remember it tomorrow!*

Action Idea: Be aware of your own language and the TV shows you see and the books you read. If you find a TV show especially bad in its use of filthy language and the wrong use of God's name, write a letter to that TV network and to the company sponsoring that show. Letters from the public are more important than most people think.

I'm old enough, Lord, to know that some things are not good for me. Help me to remember that some of the words that sound so grown-up to me are not good words. Help me to use your name only in worship and prayer because it is a holy name and not to be used in anger or surprise. Lead me so that I will not use filthy language and will not want to be around people who do.

17 Which Way Now, Lord?

Trust in the Lord with all your heart and lean not on your own understanding; in all your ways acknowledge him, and he will make your paths straight.
Proverbs 3:5-6

Because he was wise, Solomon knew that even God's people had trouble trying to understand many things that went on in the world. They especially could not understand the bad things that happened to them, their friends, and their country.

The people could not always decide by themselves what was best to do. They made mistakes and wrong decisions. But God knew everything. If the people would trust God, God would make their "paths straight," Solomon said.

When you ride your bicycle, you like the road to be straight. Straight roads, trails, and paths are much

easier to walk or ride on than hilly, curvy ones. Straight roads take you directly to the place you are going. There are no detours.

But our paths are not always straight and easy. Bad things happen to people in this world. We read about wars, crime, and hunger. We know people who are handicapped or sick. We have friends whose parents get divorced. Proverbs says we are not to trust our own understanding (or intelligence) in trying to know why these things happen, but we are to trust God.

You have many decisions to make in your life. Some are not very big decisions—like which blouse to wear to school tomorrow. Some are very big decisions though—like what you will do with your life. This verse reminds us that if we believe in God, worship him, and bring him all our problems, he will help us with our decisions; he will make our paths straight.

God may not make everything clear to you all at once, but you can be sure he is with you and will help you grow in your understanding of him. If you ask, he will direct you in the hard decisions and choices you will have to make in your life.

Nancy was in a courtroom. Her parents were getting a divorce. At first Nancy had been afraid the divorce was somehow her fault. But both her parents, and even the judge, had told her that was wrong.

Now the judge looked at Nancy. "Tomorrow you must tell me which parent you want to live with. Of course, you will still see the other one.

Nancy nodded. She still did not understand why her parents didn't want to live together anymore, but she knew she had a big choice to make.

Nancy's father was moving to Chicago where Nancy's grandparents and two uncles lived. It would be fun to live near all her cousins.

Nancy's mother's parents were dead, and she had no brothers or sisters. If Nancy stayed here with her, she could keep her same room, school, and friends.

When the judge left, Nancy's father came to her. "I love you," he said. He hugged and kissed her. "But if you decide to stay with your mother, it's OK. I only want to see you as much as I can."

"Thanks, dad."

Nancy and her mother drove home without talking. When they were inside the house, Nancy's mother put her arms around her. "You have a hard choice, Nancy. I love you very much, but I'll understand if you decide to go to Chicago. I'll want you to visit me lots, though."

"Thanks, mom."

Nancy went to her room and knelt by her bed. She told Jesus her problem, although she knew he already knew all about it. She asked Jesus to help her make the right choice. Nancy felt better then. Jesus could help her do the best thing if she trusted him.

Lying in bed that night, Nancy thought of something. In Chicago her father would be with lots of people who loved him. Her mother would be all alone if Nancy left.

"I love them both, Jesus," Nancy whispered. "But mom needs me more. I'll see daddy as much as I can and write to him every week!"

Nancy fell asleep. She knew Jesus had helped her make the right decision.

Action Idea: Do you have a friend with a problem? You may not be able to help solve it for her, but you can tell her (or write her) that you are thinking about her and praying that God will help her now. Remind her of Proverbs 3:5-6.

I want to trust you, Jesus, to help me and my friends when we have problems. I know we need you and can't find the answers for ourselves. Help me to be a friend to people who have problems, and don't let me "lean on my own understanding" when I have decisions and choices to make. Thank you for your help.

18 I Wish I Could . . .

"Do you want me to release to you the king of the Jews?" asked Pilate, knowing it was out of envy that the chief priests had handed Jesus over to him.
Mark 15:9-10

Jesus was standing in front of Pilate, on trial for his life. Pilate was the governor sent by the emperor in Rome to rule over the Jews. Pilate could have Jesus killed or set him free.

The Jewish chief priests and the leaders of the Temple had brought Jesus to Pilate because only Pilate could order anyone killed. But Pilate knew these chief priests very well. He knew why they wanted him to crucify Jesus. It was because of their envy of Jesus.

To an outsider it would sound funny to say the chief priests were envious of Jesus! Jesus was not rich like they were. He was not well educated and widely traveled as they were. Jesus was not a ruler of the Temple as they were.

But Jesus had more than money, education, and earthly power. Jesus had the love of the people. The people listened to what Jesus taught. They paid more attention to Jesus than to the Temple rulers.

Jesus did not ask the people for money. He taught them that God was like a father, that God loved them, and he loved them too.

The chief priests knew Jesus said he was the Son of God. That meant he would be above even the high priest himself. Jesus would be the one to give the orders and not them, if the people believed he was the Son of God. Out of their envy and greed, the priests wanted Jesus dead.

Envy usually leads to trouble. In this case, it led to death for Jesus and the crime of murder for the chief priests and Pilate.

Envy can cost us friendship, trust, and a good name. We sometimes wish we could do the things some of our friends can do, or have the money or good grades that others have. There is nothing wrong with wanting to be better than you are, but when envy leads to hating the person you envy, or wanting to hurt that person, then envy is very dangerous and wrong.

Wendy turned away from the list on the gym wall. She had not made the middle school basketball first team. She would not earn the big white letter B she had dreamed of.

"It's not fair!" Alicia, Wendy's best friend, said. "You're as good as that Heidi Jackson! Miss Phillips only picked her because they're both black and you're white!"

"I don't think Miss Phillips would do that," Wendy said slowly. "At least I'll be a substitute."

"But you won't get to play much if Heidi's ahead of you!"

During the morning Wendy began to wonder if Alicia could be right. There had always been friendly feelings between the black and white students and teachers, but maybe Miss Phillips didn't want an all-white team. Maybe Heidi was picked just because she was black!

"I'll fix it for you," Alicia promised.

Wendy shook her head. "No one can change Miss Phillips' mind!"

But the next day Miss Phillips said, "You're on the first team, Wendy. Heidi's sitting out for two weeks."

Wendy ran to tell Alicia.

"I know." Alicia laughed. "I did it."

Something inside warned Wendy. "How?"

"I told Miss Phillips I'd heard Heidi stayed out past curfew last night."

"Why would she do that?" Wendy asked. Everyone knew you could be benched for staying out late.

"I only told Miss Phillips I'd *heard* that," Alicia reminded her. "I didn't lie; I had my little brother say it! Heidi's mother works nights and she's alone, so she can't prove she was home. While she's benched, you can get her place on the team!"

Wendy hesitated. If she kept quiet, she would get the letter she wanted so much. *But this isn't the right way*, she thought. She took a deep breath. "I'm going to tell Miss Phillips what you heard was wrong. I'm going to ask her to put Heidi back on the first team. I'll practice harder, and maybe next year I'll get a letter! And I'll get it myself!"

Action Idea: When you feel envious of someone, stop and ask yourself what you have that others may envy you for. Maybe you can bake delicious foods, or hit a softball further than anyone in your class, or make friends with animals easily. Think of these things when you start to say, "I wish I could. . . . " Remember, you are not a copy of anyone; you are you.

I don't want to be envious of other people, Lord. I know some people will always be able to do some things better than I can, and some will own more than I do. Help me to see that what I do and who I am are the most important things to you. Lead me to be the kind of person you want me to be.

19   Let's Talk It Over

He must turn from evil and do good; he must seek peace and pursue it.

1 Peter 3:11

Peter remembered that Jesus had said "Blessed are the peacemakers." Peter remembered that Jesus said peacemakers would be called children of God. Now Peter was telling the people that they must try to bring peace to their lives and to the place where they lived.

Today we think of peacemakers as diplomats and politicians with briefcases who sit at big tables with diplomats from other nations. They talk about all the problems between their countries. They sometimes talk for months. While they talk, there is no fighting. Everyone waits to see what the peacemakers will decide.

We have had many meetings like this throughout the world in your lifetime. There are TV cameras and reporters to tell the whole world what is being said and done there. Sometimes the diplomats can talk things over, agree on what to do, and keep peace. Sometimes they cannot agree, and then there is fighting.

But Jesus and Peter were talking about what one ordinary person could do to bring peace right where that person is.

Not many people will ever have the chance to sit down and talk to other important people from a different country. Not many people will be able to help make peace between powerful nations. But a lot of us have the chance to make peace in small ways every day. Many people can help make the place they live, go to school, or work become a nicer place by helping to ease the bad feelings between people.

Peace is not easy to bring about, even in a small place. Peter says we have to "pursue" it. He meant that we would have to work hard for peace. It would not come all at once, usually, and it would not come without sacrifices on everyone's part.

Peter says the first step to peace is to stop doing the wrong thing and do the good thing instead. Only then can you start to pursue peace.

Sheila squinted into the hot Texas sun and groaned. Maria Sanchez and her friends were coming toward her across the dusty playground.

"Gringo!" Maria shouted. "Dirty gringo Sheila!"

"Don't call me that!" Sheila screamed. She turned and ran back to the school building. "Why did dad have to get transferred here for a whole year?" Sheila sobbed. "I want to be back in Indiana where everyone's like me!"

"You're a stupid wetback!" Sheila heard the cry and knew it was Megan Kramer. Megan was the leader of the Anglos in this school. There were only a few, but they stuck together.

Sheila stood at the school door to watch. Megan and her friends were lined up facing Maria and her friends. They were shouting at each other, calling names. Sheila knew they would fight if the teacher did not stop them right away. Even the boys had stopped playing ball to watch.

"It's awful here, Jesus," Sheila whispered. "I hate it! Please get dad sent back home."

"Sheila?"

Sheila turned. Jorgé Lopez was standing there. His dark face was serious, but his brown eyes were friendly. Jorgé was the only Mexican American who had spoken to Sheila and not called her "gringo."

"What do you want?" Sheila demanded.

"Peace." Jorgé did not smile. "Why can't we be friends and work together?"

"How? You call us 'gringo' and laugh at us!"

Jorgé nodded. "But you call us 'wetbacks' and laugh at us. Do you think we like that any more than you like being called 'gringo'?"

Sheila hesitated. "I guess not," she said finally.

"Then why can't we be friends?" Jorgé asked. "Or at least not enemies? I will ask Maria and all my friends to stop calling you 'gringo' if you will ask Megan and your friends to stop calling us 'wetbacks.' OK?"

Sheila smiled. "I'll try. Maybe if we can get just a few of them to stop, later everyone will."

Jorgé grinned. "Someone has to be first to make peace." He held out his hand and Sheila shook it.

Action Idea: Are there different groups in your school or neighborhood who do not get along? Can you suggest one thing they might agree to stop (or start) doing to each other to help ease the hatred and bring peace? If you cannot work directly for peace, make sure you do not take sides and add to the tension.

I'm not an important person, Lord. I can't help to bring peace between countries in the world. I'm not even important enough to stop the hatred and tension in my school. But I want to be a peacemaker. Keep me from taking sides in the arguments and fighting. Give me the courage to say that I want to have peace. Help me to be willing to pursue it, even when I can't see any results. Remind me that God will bless the peacemakers and call them his children.

20 Thanks a Lot, Lord

. . . always giving thanks to God the Father for every-thing, in the name of our Lord Jesus Christ.
Ephesians 5:20

The Christians who lived in Ephesus were excited. A fellow Christian, Tychicus, had come from Rome, where he had been with the apostle Paul. Paul was in prison in Rome, but Tychicus would tell the Christians at Ephesus how Paul was. He could tell them what Paul needed and how they could help. Best of all, he had brought a letter from Paul.

When the people of Ephesus listened to this letter, they must have shaken their heads in disbelief when they heard this verse. How could Paul say to thank God for everything? Paul was in prison! He could not come to see them himself. How could any of them thank God for that?

Giving thanks to God when things do not go the way we want them to is hard. But Paul knew that God works in ways we can't understand, and everything eventually turns out to be right when God is in charge of our lives.

It would be hard for the Ephesians to thank God for letting Paul be put in jail. But they could thank God that Paul had been with them before. They could thank God that Paul had taught them about Jesus and how Jesus wanted them to live. They could thank God that Paul had not forgotten them and was writing to them and praying for them. They could thank God that Paul had gotten to Rome where he could preach about Jesus. There were many things they could thank God for, even though it looked at first as though there was nothing to be thankful about.

Today we can thank God for Paul's being in prison in Rome. Today we know that because Paul was in a cell, he had a lot of free time. Part of this time he used to write letters like this one to the churches he had started.

If Paul had not been in prison, he might not have had the time to write so many letters. We would not have them to read in our Bibles today. We would not have had their descriptions of the early church to help us understand how it grew. We would not have their instructions to guide us as Christians.

Tammy had mononucleosis. The doctor said she would have to stay in bed for several weeks. She had watched TV and read, but now Tammy was tired of both.

"I wish I could be back with my friends," she told her mother.

"Mrs. Rogers said that when I visited her at the nursing home. She says not many people come to see her or even call on the phone."

"I remember when I was little and she led the Cherub Choir," Tammy said. "She was really nice, even when the big boys goofed off at practice." Tammy glanced at the telephone by her bed. "I could call her, but what would we talk about?"

"Ask how she is and if she remembers the Cherub Choir," Tammy's mother advised. "I'm sure it will go all right from there."

It took Tammy a minute to make Mrs. Rogers understand who she was. Then the old woman sobbed. "Oh, Tammy, I'm sorry you're sick, but it's so nice to get a phone call! Of course I remember you and the Cherub Choir!"

When she finally hung up, Tammy noticed that she and Mrs. Rogers had talked almost a half hour! It had not been hard at all!

"I could call some other people," Tammy told her mother. "Or write some letters."

By the next day Tammy had a list of 10 people from the church who were shut-in and would like a telephone call. She decided to call three each day, then start the list over.

When Tammy was better, she was surprised at how fast the time had gone. She was also surprised at all the new friends she had made.

"Being sick made me understand how people feel when they can't get out of the house," she told her mother. "I guess I should thank God for giving me the chance to get to know so many people from the church—even if I had to get sick to do it!"

Action Idea: Think of all the things you can thank God for today. Think of things to be thankful for, even if they do not seem like good things. If someone in your house is sick, thank God for doctors, hospitals, and medicines. If you got a bad grade today, thank God for the good grades you've had before. Practice thinking of things to be thankful for everyday.

Thank you, God, for always being with me. Thank you for all the good things that happen to me, my family, and my friends. I know I usually take these good things for granted and forget to thank you for them. When something happens that I don't like, help me to remember that you make everything work together so good things will happen to those who believe in you.

21   It Wasn't Just Me

Humble yourselves before the Lord, and he will lift you up.

James 4:10

The Bible talks a lot about being humble. Being humble, or having humility, means the opposite of being proud and boastful.

Jesus often accused the religious leaders of his day of being proud and arrogant. These men liked the attention people gave them, but many of them did not love God or really care about other people.

Proud people are not humble before God. They are doing well and think they are doing it all by themselves. They see no need to change anything about themselves. They don't mind bragging to get others to admire and perhaps envy them.

Naturally you should be proud of the outstanding things you have done. You should be proud of getting

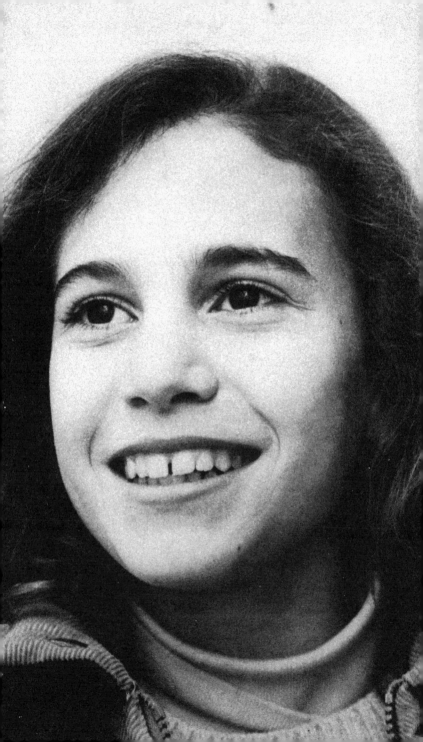

an A in English or winning a medal at a track meet or earning a perfect attendance pin at Sunday school. You should be happy when you earn recognition and people congratulate you.

But Christians know they have not done anything entirely on their own abilities and power. They thank God for their talents and skills. They do not boast about how great they are.

Often Christians are not the ones who seem most successful. They may be the members of the chorus who don't get to sing solos, the substitutes on the team, and the ones who never make the honor roll. What does this verse mean if you are one of these Christians?

James divided the verse into two parts. The first part tells what you should do: humble yourself before the Lord. That means to tell Jesus your problems and dreams. Tell him you know you can't do it on your own. Ask for his help.

The second part of this verse tells us what the Lord will do: lift you up. James is not saying God will make everything perfect in a split second, like magic. Lifting you up means that God will be with you and help you. And God will love you whether you do anything special or not.

Shelley opened her grade card and smiled. The C she had gotten last time in math was up to a B now.

"I know I got all A's without looking," Julie Stans said. "I always get all A's."

"And you're always bragging about it!" snapped Steve Preston.

"Yeah," Nathan Hodges added. "How come you have to act like you're better than everyone else?"

"Because I am!" Julie tossed her head and walked away.

Shelley watched as Julie sat down alone at one side of the playground. She took out a book and began to read.

She may get the best grades, but she doesn't act happy, Shelley thought.

That night Shelley's mother and father smiled when they saw her grades. "These are wonderful, honey!" Shelley's father said as he gave her a hug.

"You should be Julie's dad," Shelley said. "She gets all A's. You should have heard her bragging about it today—as usual! She brags about every little thing she does!"

"How well do you know Julie?" Shelley's mother asked.

Shelley shrugged. "She's been in my class since she moved here a couple months ago. But I don't hang out with her."

"Then you don't know her father left them last year. Her mother moved them here. She works the same shift as I do at the hospital, but she has to have another part-time job to support Julie and her brother. She isn't home much."

"I didn't know that." Shelley said. She thought for a minute. "Do you mean Julie brags so much

104

to—well, sort of make up for not having her dad and for her mother working so much?"

"Maybe," Shelley's mother said. "What do you think?"

"None of the kids knows about her mom and dad," Shelley said slowly. "No one likes Julie 'cause she's always bragging. But maybe if we were friends with her—"

Shelley stopped. It might not help Julie, but she wouldn't know if she didn't try. Tomorrow she would congratulate Julie on her grades, and ask her to sit with the gang at lunch.

Action Idea: The next time someone compliments you, thank them. Then try to give them a compliment, too. It does not have to be something big and important. You could say you like that person's sense of humor, her quiet voice, or smile. This way you'll be helping her and also humbling yourself before God.

I know that I don't really do anything entirely on my own, Lord. Sometimes it's hard to be humble when people make a big fuss over what I've done. Help me to remember that you gave me my talents and skills. I especially thank you for (you put in your biggest talent or gift). I want to use it and my other talents for your glory. Help me to stay humble and trust you to lift me up.

22 What a Neat Place

For by him all things were created: things in heaven and earth, visible and invisible . . . .

Colossians 1:16

In this verse Paul reminds us that everything in our world was created by God. Genesis says that when God looked over what he had created, God said that it was good. But human beings have not always treated God's good creation carefully. Often what we do to our world causes more harm than good.

Jesus talked a lot about things in nature. Many of the stories he told were about what the people could see around them.

Jesus talked about the flowers. He told the disciples that even great King Solomon had not looked as beautiful as the flowers, even in his best and most expensive clothes.

Jesus talked about the fields and what grew there. He told a story about a man planting seeds and what happened to the seeds that did not fall on good ground.

Jesus talked about the birds. He told the people that God knew when even the smallest bird died; and that God loved the people more than the birds.

Jesus talked about the waters, the skies, and the weather. Once he calmed the waves and wind while he and his disciples were crossing the lake in a small boat.

In those days people walked places much more than we do. Jesus and his disciples walked everywhere. They walked along the lake shores, on the desert, and in the hills. They saw the shepherds with their sheep. They saw the farmers planting and harvesting their crops. They saw the land in the sun and in the rain. They slept outside most nights where they could see the stars and moon high above them.

Jesus understood that all of nature was God's creation. He knew God loved all that he had made. Jesus respected what God had made because God had made it. Jesus took care of what God had given to human beings.

Debbie was excited. Her family was going to camp at the lake for a whole week. Debbie loved the lake. She liked watching the birds that walked so funny on the beach. She liked seeing the moon reflected on the water at night. She liked seeing the gentle shadows the leaves of the trees made on the tent roof early in the morning.

But when Debbie's family got to the lake there were no empty camp sites.

Debbie's father talked to the ranger. "We can't camp in the regular area tonight," he said when he came back. "But we can put our tent up in the picnic area. It'll be just as nice."

At first Debbie was happy about camping in a different part of the park. Then she saw the picnic area. Pop cans and garbage were scattered everywhere.

"Mom, it's terrible!" Debbie felt like crying. "I don't want to camp here!"

Her mother nodded. "The people who ate here forgot this is part of God's creation and should be kept beautiful."

"We can clean it up again," Debbie's father said. "We'll each take a plastic bag, and when we've picked up this trash, it will be as pretty as ever."

Debbie didn't like the idea of picking up someone else's trash, but she helped anyway. She put all the cans in her bag while her parents put the other things in their bags. In a short time the area was clean again. The site looked ready for a tent and campers.

"See?" Debbie's father smiled at her. "We've helped make God's world pretty again. I'm sure God is happy we helped make it look the way God made it. We'll put our trash in the cans where it belongs. Then this site will stay beautiful all the time we're here."

Debbie laughed. "I never thought of picking up trash as helping God, but it is, isn't it? Maybe I can find some other places to clean up while we're here."

Action Idea: Do you know a place that needs to be cleaned up? You can help make places around you look nicer by picking up trash. You can keep it nice by not littering. If you have the owner's permission, you can plant flower seeds. Ask some of your friends to help with the clean-up. You may find enough aluminum cans to earn money at a recycling plant.

Dear God, I know you want us to respect all of nature and to keep it in good condition. Help me to remember that you love every animal in the world. Help me to remember not to hurt anything you have made. Thank you for all the beautiful things you have put on earth for us to use and enjoy.